Firearm Log Book

Name:
Telephone Number:
Address:

Contents

Manufacturer & Type:	Unique Identifiers:	Page Number:

Contents

Manufacturer & Type:	Unique Identifiers:	Page Number:

Contents

Manufacturer & Type:	Unique Identifiers:	Page Number:

Contents

Manufacturer & Type:	Unique Identifiers:	Page Number:

Contents

Manufacturer & Type:	Unique Identifiers:	Page Number:

Contents

Manufacturer & Type:	Unique Identifiers:	Page Number:

Contents

Manufacturer & Type:	Unique Identifiers:	Page Number:

Contents

Manufacturer & Type:	Unique Identifiers:	Page Number:

Manufacturer & Type:		Model:	Serial Number:
Alterations:		Capacity:	Caliber
Importer:		Barrel:	Action:
Notes:			

AQUIRED	Date:	SOLD	Date:
Cost:	From:	Cost:	To:
Notes:		Notes:	

Manufacturer & Type:		Model:	Serial Number:
Alterations:		Capacity:	Caliber
Importer:		Barrel:	Action:
Notes:			

AQUIRED	Date:	SOLD	Date:
Cost:	From:	Cost:	To:
Notes:		Notes:	

Manufacturer & Type:		Model:	Serial Number:
Alterations:		Capacity:	Caliber
Importer:		Barrel:	Action:

Notes:

AQUIRED	Date:	SOLD	Date:
Cost:	From:	Cost:	To:
Notes:		Notes:	

Manufacturer & Type:		Model:	Serial Number:
Alterations:		Capacity:	Caliber
Importer:		Barrel:	Action:

Notes:

AQUIRED	Date:	SOLD	Date:
Cost:	From:	Cost:	To:
Notes:		Notes:	

Manufacturer & Type:		Model:	Serial Number:
Alterations:		Capacity:	Caliber
Importer:		Barrel:	Action:

Notes:

AQUIRED	Date:	SOLD	Date:
Cost:	From:	Cost:	To:
Notes:		Notes:	

Manufacturer & Type:		Model:	Serial Number:
Alterations:		Capacity:	Caliber
Importer:		Barrel:	Action:

Notes:

AQUIRED	Date:	SOLD	Date:
Cost:	From:	Cost:	To:
Notes:		Notes:	

Manufacturer & Type:		Model:	Serial Number:
Alterations:		Capacity:	Caliber
Importer:		Barrel:	Action:

Notes:

AQUIRED	Date:	SOLD	Date:
Cost:	From:	Cost:	To:
Notes:		Notes:	

Manufacturer & Type:		Model:	Serial Number:
Alterations:		Capacity:	Caliber
Importer:		Barrel:	Action:

Notes:

AQUIRED	Date:	SOLD	Date:
Cost:	From:	Cost:	To:
Notes:		Notes:	

Manufacturer & Type:		Model:	Serial Number:
Alterations:		Capacity:	Caliber
Importer:		Barrel:	Action:
Notes:			

AQUIRED	Date:	SOLD	Date:
Cost:	From:	Cost:	To:
Notes:		Notes:	

Manufacturer & Type:		Model:	Serial Number:
Alterations:		Capacity:	Caliber
Importer:		Barrel:	Action:
Notes:			

AQUIRED	Date:	SOLD	Date:
Cost:	From:	Cost:	To:
Notes:		Notes:	

Manufacturer & Type:		Model:	Serial Number:
Alterations:		Capacity:	Caliber
Importer:		Barrel:	Action:
Notes:			

AQUIRED	Date:	SOLD	Date:
Cost:	From:	Cost:	To:
Notes:		Notes:	

Manufacturer & Type:		Model:	Serial Number:
Alterations:		Capacity:	Caliber
Importer:		Barrel:	Action:
Notes:			

AQUIRED	Date:	SOLD	Date:
Cost:	From:	Cost:	To:
Notes:		Notes:	

Manufacturer & Type:		Model:	Serial Number:
Alterations:		Capacity:	Caliber
Importer:		Barrel:	Action:
Notes:			

AQUIRED	Date:	SOLD	Date:
Cost:	From:	Cost:	To:
Notes:		Notes:	

Manufacturer & Type:		Model:	Serial Number:
Alterations:		Capacity:	Caliber
Importer:		Barrel:	Action:
Notes:			

AQUIRED	Date:	SOLD	Date:
Cost:	From:	Cost:	To:
Notes:		Notes:	

Manufacturer & Type:		Model:	Serial Number:
Alterations:		Capacity:	Caliber
Importer:		Barrel:	Action:

Notes:

AQUIRED	Date:	SOLD	Date:
Cost:	From:	Cost:	To:
Notes:		Notes:	

Manufacturer & Type:		Model:	Serial Number:
Alterations:		Capacity:	Caliber
Importer:		Barrel:	Action:

Notes:

AQUIRED	Date:	SOLD	Date:
Cost:	From:	Cost:	To:
Notes:		Notes:	

Manufacturer & Type:		Model:	Serial Number:
Alterations:		Capacity:	Caliber
Importer:		Barrel:	Action:

Notes:

AQUIRED	Date:	SOLD	Date:
Cost:	From:	Cost:	To:
Notes:		Notes:	

Manufacturer & Type:		Model:	Serial Number:
Alterations:		Capacity:	Caliber
Importer:		Barrel:	Action:

Notes:

AQUIRED	Date:	SOLD	Date:
Cost:	From:	Cost:	To:
Notes:		Notes:	

Manufacturer & Type:		Model:	Serial Number:
Alterations:		Capacity:	Caliber
Importer:		Barrel:	Action:

Notes:

AQUIRED	Date:	SOLD	Date:
Cost:	From:	Cost:	To:
Notes:		Notes:	

Manufacturer & Type:		Model:	Serial Number:
Alterations:		Capacity:	Caliber
Importer:		Barrel:	Action:

Notes:

AQUIRED	Date:	SOLD	Date:
Cost:	From:	Cost:	To:
Notes:		Notes:	

Manufacturer & Type:		Model:	Serial Number:
Alterations:		Capacity:	Caliber
Importer:		Barrel:	Action:
Notes:			

AQUIRED	Date:	SOLD	Date:
Cost:	From:	Cost:	To:
Notes:		Notes:	

Manufacturer & Type:		Model:	Serial Number:
Alterations:		Capacity:	Caliber
Importer:		Barrel:	Action:
Notes:			

AQUIRED	Date:	SOLD	Date:
Cost:	From:	Cost:	To:
Notes:		Notes:	

Manufacturer & Type:		Model:	Serial Number:
Alterations:		Capacity:	Caliber
Importer:		Barrel:	Action:

Notes:

AQUIRED	Date:	SOLD	Date:
Cost:	From:	Cost:	To:
Notes:		Notes:	

Manufacturer & Type:		Model:	Serial Number:
Alterations:		Capacity:	Caliber
Importer:		Barrel:	Action:

Notes:

AQUIRED	Date:	SOLD	Date:
Cost:	From:	Cost:	To:
Notes:		Notes:	

Manufacturer & Type:		Model:	Serial Number:
Alterations:		Capacity:	Caliber
Importer:		Barrel:	Action:

Notes:

AQUIRED	Date:	SOLD	Date:
Cost:	From:	Cost:	To:
Notes:		Notes:	

Manufacturer & Type:		Model:	Serial Number:
Alterations:		Capacity:	Caliber
Importer:		Barrel:	Action:

Notes:

AQUIRED	Date:	SOLD	Date:
Cost:	From:	Cost:	To:
Notes:		Notes:	

Manufacturer & Type:		Model:	Serial Number:
Alterations:		Capacity:	Caliber
Importer:		Barrel:	Action:

Notes:

AQUIRED	Date:	SOLD	Date:
Cost:	From:	Cost:	To:
Notes:		Notes:	

Manufacturer & Type:		Model:	Serial Number:
Alterations:		Capacity:	Caliber
Importer:		Barrel:	Action:

Notes:

AQUIRED	Date:	SOLD	Date:
Cost:	From:	Cost:	To:
Notes:		Notes:	

Manufacturer & Type:		Model:	Serial Number:
Alterations:		Capacity:	Caliber
Importer:		Barrel:	Action:

Notes:

AQUIRED	Date:	SOLD	Date:
Cost:	From:	Cost:	To:
Notes:		Notes:	

Manufacturer & Type:		Model:	Serial Number:
Alterations:		Capacity:	Caliber
Importer:		Barrel:	Action:

Notes:

AQUIRED	Date:	SOLD	Date:
Cost:	From:	Cost:	To:
Notes:		Notes:	

Manufacturer & Type:		Model:	Serial Number:
Alterations:		Capacity:	Caliber
Importer:		Barrel:	Action:

Notes:

AQUIRED	Date:	SOLD	Date:
Cost:	From:	Cost:	To:
Notes:		Notes:	

Manufacturer & Type:		Model:	Serial Number:
Alterations:		Capacity:	Caliber
Importer:		Barrel:	Action:

Notes:

AQUIRED	Date:	SOLD	Date:
Cost:	From:	Cost:	To:
Notes:		Notes:	

Manufacturer & Type:		Model:	Serial Number:
Alterations:		Capacity:	Caliber
Importer:		Barrel:	Action:
Notes:			

AQUIRED	Date:	SOLD	Date:
Cost:	From:	Cost:	To:
Notes:		Notes:	

Manufacturer & Type:		Model:	Serial Number:
Alterations:		Capacity:	Caliber
Importer:		Barrel:	Action:
Notes:			

AQUIRED	Date:	SOLD	Date:
Cost:	From:	Cost:	To:
Notes:		Notes:	

Manufacturer & Type:		Model:	Serial Number:
Alterations:		Capacity:	Caliber
Importer:		Barrel:	Action:
Notes:			

AQUIRED	Date:	SOLD	Date:
Cost:	From:	Cost:	To:
Notes:		Notes:	

Manufacturer & Type:		Model:	Serial Number:
Alterations:		Capacity:	Caliber
Importer:		Barrel:	Action:
Notes:			

AQUIRED	Date:	SOLD	Date:
Cost:	From:	Cost:	To:
Notes:		Notes:	

Manufacturer & Type:		Model:	Serial Number:
Alterations:		Capacity:	Caliber
Importer:		Barrel:	Action:

Notes:

AQUIRED	Date:	SOLD	Date:
Cost:	From:	Cost:	To:
Notes:		Notes:	

Manufacturer & Type:		Model:	Serial Number:
Alterations:		Capacity:	Caliber
Importer:		Barrel:	Action:

Notes:

AQUIRED	Date:	SOLD	Date:
Cost:	From:	Cost:	To:
Notes:		Notes:	

Manufacturer & Type:		Model:	Serial Number:
Alterations:		Capacity:	Caliber
Importer:		Barrel:	Action:

Notes:

AQUIRED	Date:	SOLD	Date:
Cost:	From:	Cost:	To:
Notes:		Notes:	

Manufacturer & Type:		Model:	Serial Number:
Alterations:		Capacity:	Caliber
Importer:		Barrel:	Action:

Notes:

AQUIRED	Date:	SOLD	Date:
Cost:	From:	Cost:	To:
Notes:		Notes:	

Manufacturer & Type:		Model:	Serial Number:
Alterations:		Capacity:	Caliber
Importer:		Barrel:	Action:
Notes:			

AQUIRED	Date:	SOLD	Date:
Cost:	From:	Cost:	To:
Notes:		Notes:	

Manufacturer & Type:		Model:	Serial Number:
Alterations:		Capacity:	Caliber
Importer:		Barrel:	Action:
Notes:			

AQUIRED	Date:	SOLD	Date:
Cost:	From:	Cost:	To:
Notes:		Notes:	

Manufacturer & Type:		Model:	Serial Number:
Alterations:		Capacity:	Caliber
Importer:		Barrel:	Action:

Notes:

AQUIRED	Date:	SOLD	Date:
Cost:	From:	Cost:	To:
Notes:		Notes:	

Manufacturer & Type:		Model:	Serial Number:
Alterations:		Capacity:	Caliber
Importer:		Barrel:	Action:

Notes:

AQUIRED	Date:	SOLD	Date:
Cost:	From:	Cost:	To:
Notes:		Notes:	

Manufacturer & Type:		Model:	Serial Number:
Alterations:		Capacity:	Caliber
Importer:		Barrel:	Action:

Notes:

AQUIRED	Date:	SOLD	Date:
Cost:	From:	Cost:	To:
Notes:		Notes:	

Manufacturer & Type:		Model:	Serial Number:
Alterations:		Capacity:	Caliber
Importer:		Barrel:	Action:

Notes:

AQUIRED	Date:	SOLD	Date:
Cost:	From:	Cost:	To:
Notes:		Notes:	

Manufacturer & Type:		Model:	Serial Number:
Alterations:		Capacity:	Caliber
Importer:		Barrel:	Action:
Notes:			

AQUIRED	Date:	SOLD	Date:
Cost:	From:	Cost:	To:
Notes:		Notes:	

Manufacturer & Type:		Model:	Serial Number:
Alterations:		Capacity:	Caliber
Importer:		Barrel:	Action:
Notes:			

AQUIRED	Date:	SOLD	Date:
Cost:	From:	Cost:	To:
Notes:		Notes:	

Manufacturer & Type:		Model:	Serial Number:
Alterations:		Capacity:	Caliber
Importer:		Barrel:	Action:
Notes:			

AQUIRED	Date:	SOLD	Date:
Cost:	From:	Cost:	To:
Notes:		Notes:	

Manufacturer & Type:		Model:	Serial Number:
Alterations:		Capacity:	Caliber
Importer:		Barrel:	Action:
Notes:			

AQUIRED	Date:	SOLD	Date:
Cost:	From:	Cost:	To:
Notes:		Notes:	

Manufacturer & Type:		Model:	Serial Number:
Alterations:		Capacity:	Caliber
Importer:		Barrel:	Action:

Notes:

AQUIRED	Date:	SOLD	Date:
Cost:	From:	Cost:	To:
Notes:		Notes:	

Manufacturer & Type:		Model:	Serial Number:
Alterations:		Capacity:	Caliber
Importer:		Barrel:	Action:

Notes:

AQUIRED	Date:	SOLD	Date:
Cost:	From:	Cost:	To:
Notes:		Notes:	

Manufacturer & Type:	Model:	Serial Number:
Alterations:	Capacity:	Caliber
Importer:	Barrel:	Action:

Notes:

AQUIRED	Date:	SOLD	Date:
Cost:	From:	Cost:	To:
Notes:		Notes:	

Manufacturer & Type:	Model:	Serial Number:
Alterations:	Capacity:	Caliber
Importer:	Barrel:	Action:

Notes:

AQUIRED	Date:	SOLD	Date:
Cost:	From:	Cost:	To:
Notes:		Notes:	

Manufacturer & Type:		Model:	Serial Number:
Alterations:		Capacity:	Caliber
Importer:		Barrel:	Action:

Notes:

AQUIRED	Date:	SOLD	Date:
Cost:	From:	Cost:	To:
Notes:		Notes:	

Manufacturer & Type:		Model:	Serial Number:
Alterations:		Capacity:	Caliber
Importer:		Barrel:	Action:

Notes:

AQUIRED	Date:	SOLD	Date:
Cost:	From:	Cost:	To:
Notes:		Notes:	

Manufacturer & Type:		Model:	Serial Number:
Alterations:		Capacity:	Caliber
Importer:		Barrel:	Action:
Notes:			

AQUIRED	Date:	SOLD	Date:
Cost:	From:	Cost:	To:
Notes:		Notes:	

Manufacturer & Type:		Model:	Serial Number:
Alterations:		Capacity:	Caliber
Importer:		Barrel:	Action:
Notes:			

AQUIRED	Date:	SOLD	Date:
Cost:	From:	Cost:	To:
Notes:		Notes:	

Manufacturer & Type:		Model:	Serial Number:
Alterations:		Capacity:	Caliber
Importer:		Barrel:	Action:

Notes:

AQUIRED	Date:	SOLD	Date:
Cost:	From:	Cost:	To:
Notes:		Notes:	

Manufacturer & Type:		Model:	Serial Number:
Alterations:		Capacity:	Caliber
Importer:		Barrel:	Action:

Notes:

AQUIRED	Date:	SOLD	Date:
Cost:	From:	Cost:	To:
Notes:		Notes:	

Manufacturer & Type:		Model:	Serial Number:
Alterations:		Capacity:	Caliber
Importer:		Barrel:	Action:

Notes:

AQUIRED	Date:	SOLD	Date:
Cost:	From:	Cost:	To:
Notes:		Notes:	

Manufacturer & Type:		Model:	Serial Number:
Alterations:		Capacity:	Caliber
Importer:		Barrel:	Action:

Notes:

AQUIRED	Date:	SOLD	Date:
Cost:	From:	Cost:	To:
Notes:		Notes:	

Manufacturer & Type:		Model:	Serial Number:
Alterations:		Capacity:	Caliber
Importer:		Barrel:	Action:
Notes:			

AQUIRED	Date:	SOLD	Date:
Cost:	From:	Cost:	To:
Notes:		Notes:	

Manufacturer & Type:		Model:	Serial Number:
Alterations:		Capacity:	Caliber
Importer:		Barrel:	Action:
Notes:			

AQUIRED	Date:	SOLD	Date:
Cost:	From:	Cost:	To:
Notes:		Notes:	

Manufacturer & Type:		Model:	Serial Number:
Alterations:		Capacity:	Caliber
Importer:		Barrel:	Action:

Notes:

AQUIRED	Date:	SOLD	Date:
Cost:	From:	Cost:	To:
Notes:		Notes:	

Manufacturer & Type:		Model:	Serial Number:
Alterations:		Capacity:	Caliber
Importer:		Barrel:	Action:

Notes:

AQUIRED	Date:	SOLD	Date:
Cost:	From:	Cost:	To:
Notes:		Notes:	

Manufacturer & Type:		Model:	Serial Number:
Alterations:		Capacity:	Caliber
Importer:		Barrel:	Action:

Notes:

AQUIRED	Date:	SOLD	Date:
Cost:	From:	Cost:	To:
Notes:		Notes:	

Manufacturer & Type:		Model:	Serial Number:
Alterations:		Capacity:	Caliber
Importer:		Barrel:	Action:

Notes:

AQUIRED	Date:	SOLD	Date:
Cost:	From:	Cost:	To:
Notes:		Notes:	

Manufacturer & Type:		Model:	Serial Number:
Alterations:		Capacity:	Caliber
Importer:		Barrel:	Action:
Notes:			

AQUIRED	Date:	SOLD	Date:
Cost:	From:	Cost:	To:
Notes:		Notes:	

Manufacturer & Type:		Model:	Serial Number:
Alterations:		Capacity:	Caliber
Importer:		Barrel:	Action:
Notes:			

AQUIRED	Date:	SOLD	Date:
Cost:	From:	Cost:	To:
Notes:		Notes:	

Manufacturer & Type:		Model:	Serial Number:
Alterations:		Capacity:	Caliber
Importer:		Barrel:	Action:
Notes:			

AQUIRED	Date:	SOLD	Date:
Cost:	From:	Cost:	To:
Notes:		Notes:	

Manufacturer & Type:		Model:	Serial Number:
Alterations:		Capacity:	Caliber
Importer:		Barrel:	Action:
Notes:			

AQUIRED	Date:	SOLD	Date:
Cost:	From:	Cost:	To:
Notes:		Notes:	

Manufacturer & Type:		Model:	Serial Number:
Alterations:		Capacity:	Caliber
Importer:		Barrel:	Action:

Notes:

AQUIRED	Date:	SOLD	Date:
Cost:	From:	Cost:	To:
Notes:		Notes:	

Manufacturer & Type:		Model:	Serial Number:
Alterations:		Capacity:	Caliber
Importer:		Barrel:	Action:

Notes:

AQUIRED	Date:	SOLD	Date:
Cost:	From:	Cost:	To:
Notes:		Notes:	

Manufacturer & Type:		Model:	Serial Number:
Alterations:		Capacity:	Caliber
Importer:		Barrel:	Action:

Notes:

AQUIRED	Date:	SOLD	Date:
Cost:	From:	Cost:	To:
Notes:		Notes:	

Manufacturer & Type:		Model:	Serial Number:
Alterations:		Capacity:	Caliber
Importer:		Barrel:	Action:

Notes:

AQUIRED	Date:	SOLD	Date:
Cost:	From:	Cost:	To:
Notes:		Notes:	

Manufacturer & Type:		Model:	Serial Number:
Alterations:		Capacity:	Caliber
Importer:		Barrel:	Action:

Notes:

AQUIRED	Date:	SOLD	Date:
Cost:	From:	Cost:	To:
Notes:		Notes:	

Manufacturer & Type:		Model:	Serial Number:
Alterations:		Capacity:	Caliber
Importer:		Barrel:	Action:

Notes:

AQUIRED	Date:	SOLD	Date:
Cost:	From:	Cost:	To:
Notes:		Notes:	

Manufacturer & Type:		Model:	Serial Number:
Alterations:		Capacity:	Caliber
Importer:		Barrel:	Action:
Notes:			

AQUIRED	Date:	SOLD	Date:
Cost:	From:	Cost:	To:
Notes:		Notes:	

Manufacturer & Type:		Model:	Serial Number:
Alterations:		Capacity:	Caliber
Importer:		Barrel:	Action:
Notes:			

AQUIRED	Date:	SOLD	Date:
Cost:	From:	Cost:	To:
Notes:		Notes:	

Manufacturer & Type:		Model:	Serial Number:
Alterations:		Capacity:	Caliber
Importer:		Barrel:	Action:

Notes:

AQUIRED	Date:	SOLD	Date:
Cost:	From:	Cost:	To:
Notes:		Notes:	

Manufacturer & Type:		Model:	Serial Number:
Alterations:		Capacity:	Caliber
Importer:		Barrel:	Action:

Notes:

AQUIRED	Date:	SOLD	Date:
Cost:	From:	Cost:	To:
Notes:		Notes:	

Manufacturer & Type:		Model:	Serial Number:
Alterations:		Capacity:	Caliber
Importer:		Barrel:	Action:

Notes:

AQUIRED	Date:	SOLD	Date:
Cost:	From:	Cost:	To:
Notes:		Notes:	

Manufacturer & Type:		Model:	Serial Number:
Alterations:		Capacity:	Caliber
Importer:		Barrel:	Action:

Notes:

AQUIRED	Date:	SOLD	Date:
Cost:	From:	Cost:	To:
Notes:		Notes:	

Manufacturer & Type:	Model:	Serial Number:
Alterations:	Capacity:	Caliber
Importer:	Barrel:	Action:

Notes:

AQUIRED	Date:	SOLD	Date:
Cost:	From:	Cost:	To:
Notes:		Notes:	

Manufacturer & Type:	Model:	Serial Number:
Alterations:	Capacity:	Caliber
Importer:	Barrel:	Action:

Notes:

AQUIRED	Date:	SOLD	Date:
Cost:	From:	Cost:	To:
Notes:		Notes:	

Manufacturer & Type:		Model:	Serial Number:
Alterations:		Capacity:	Caliber
Importer:		Barrel:	Action:
Notes:			

AQUIRED	Date:	SOLD	Date:
Cost:	From:	Cost:	To:
Notes:		Notes:	

Manufacturer & Type:		Model:	Serial Number:
Alterations:		Capacity:	Caliber
Importer:		Barrel:	Action:
Notes:			

AQUIRED	Date:	SOLD	Date:
Cost:	From:	Cost:	To:
Notes:		Notes:	

Manufacturer & Type:		Model:	Serial Number:
Alterations:		Capacity:	Caliber
Importer:		Barrel:	Action:

Notes:

AQUIRED	Date:	SOLD	Date:
Cost:	From:	Cost:	To:
Notes:		Notes:	

Manufacturer & Type:		Model:	Serial Number:
Alterations:		Capacity:	Caliber
Importer:		Barrel:	Action:

Notes:

AQUIRED	Date:	SOLD	Date:
Cost:	From:	Cost:	To:
Notes:		Notes:	

Manufacturer & Type:		Model:	Serial Number:
Alterations:		Capacity:	Caliber
Importer:		Barrel:	Action:

Notes:

AQUIRED	Date:	SOLD	Date:
Cost:	From:	Cost:	To:
Notes:		Notes:	

Manufacturer & Type:		Model:	Serial Number:
Alterations:		Capacity:	Caliber
Importer:		Barrel:	Action:

Notes:

AQUIRED	Date:	SOLD	Date:
Cost:	From:	Cost:	To:
Notes:		Notes:	

Manufacturer & Type:		Model:	Serial Number:
Alterations:		Capacity:	Caliber
Importer:		Barrel:	Action:

Notes:

AQUIRED	Date:	SOLD	Date:
Cost:	From:	Cost:	To:
Notes:		Notes:	

Manufacturer & Type:		Model:	Serial Number:
Alterations:		Capacity:	Caliber
Importer:		Barrel:	Action:

Notes:

AQUIRED	Date:	SOLD	Date:
Cost:	From:	Cost:	To:
Notes:		Notes:	

Manufacturer & Type:		Model:	Serial Number:
Alterations:		Capacity:	Caliber
Importer:		Barrel:	Action:
Notes:			

AQUIRED	Date:	SOLD	Date:
Cost:	From:	Cost:	To:
Notes:		Notes:	

Manufacturer & Type:		Model:	Serial Number:
Alterations:		Capacity:	Caliber
Importer:		Barrel:	Action:
Notes:			

AQUIRED	Date:	SOLD	Date:
Cost:	From:	Cost:	To:
Notes:		Notes:	

Manufacturer & Type:		Model:	Serial Number:
Alterations:		Capacity:	Caliber
Importer:		Barrel:	Action:

Notes:

AQUIRED	Date:	SOLD	Date:
Cost:	From:	Cost:	To:
Notes:		Notes:	

Manufacturer & Type:		Model:	Serial Number:
Alterations:		Capacity:	Caliber
Importer:		Barrel:	Action:

Notes:

AQUIRED	Date:	SOLD	Date:
Cost:	From:	Cost:	To:
Notes:		Notes:	

Manufacturer & Type:	Model:	Serial Number:
Alterations:	Capacity:	Caliber
Importer:	Barrel:	Action:

Notes:

AQUIRED	Date:	SOLD	Date:
Cost:	From:	Cost:	To:
Notes:		Notes:	

Manufacturer & Type:	Model:	Serial Number:
Alterations:	Capacity:	Caliber
Importer:	Barrel:	Action:

Notes:

AQUIRED	Date:	SOLD	Date:
Cost:	From:	Cost:	To:
Notes:		Notes:	

Manufacturer & Type:		Model:	Serial Number:
Alterations:		Capacity:	Caliber
Importer:		Barrel:	Action:

Notes:

AQUIRED	Date:	SOLD	Date:
Cost:	From:	Cost:	To:
Notes:		Notes:	

Manufacturer & Type:		Model:	Serial Number:
Alterations:		Capacity:	Caliber
Importer:		Barrel:	Action:

Notes:

AQUIRED	Date:	SOLD	Date:
Cost:	From:	Cost:	To:
Notes:		Notes:	

Manufacturer & Type:	Model:	Serial Number:
Alterations:	Capacity:	Caliber
Importer:	Barrel:	Action:

Notes:

AQUIRED	Date:	SOLD	Date:
Cost:	From:	Cost:	To:
Notes:		Notes:	

Manufacturer & Type:	Model:	Serial Number:
Alterations:	Capacity:	Caliber
Importer:	Barrel:	Action:

Notes:

AQUIRED	Date:	SOLD	Date:
Cost:	From:	Cost:	To:
Notes:		Notes:	

Manufacturer & Type:		Model:	Serial Number:
Alterations:		Capacity:	Caliber
Importer:		Barrel:	Action:

Notes:

AQUIRED	Date:	SOLD	Date:
Cost:	From:	Cost:	To:
Notes:		Notes:	

Manufacturer & Type:		Model:	Serial Number:
Alterations:		Capacity:	Caliber
Importer:		Barrel:	Action:

Notes:

AQUIRED	Date:	SOLD	Date:
Cost:	From:	Cost:	To:
Notes:		Notes:	

Manufacturer & Type:		Model:	Serial Number:
Alterations:		Capacity:	Caliber
Importer:		Barrel:	Action:
Notes:			

AQUIRED	Date:	SOLD	Date:
Cost:	From:	Cost:	To:
Notes:		Notes:	

Manufacturer & Type:		Model:	Serial Number:
Alterations:		Capacity:	Caliber
Importer:		Barrel:	Action:
Notes:			

AQUIRED	Date:	SOLD	Date:
Cost:	From:	Cost:	To:
Notes:		Notes:	

Manufacturer & Type:		Model:	Serial Number:
Alterations:		Capacity:	Caliber
Importer:		Barrel:	Action:

Notes:

AQUIRED	Date:	SOLD	Date:
Cost:	From:	Cost:	To:
Notes:		Notes:	

Manufacturer & Type:		Model:	Serial Number:
Alterations:		Capacity:	Caliber
Importer:		Barrel:	Action:

Notes:

AQUIRED	Date:	SOLD	Date:
Cost:	From:	Cost:	To:
Notes:		Notes:	

Manufacturer & Type:		Model:	Serial Number:
Alterations:		Capacity:	Caliber
Importer:		Barrel:	Action:

Notes:

AQUIRED	Date:	SOLD	Date:
Cost:	From:	Cost:	To:
Notes:		Notes:	

Manufacturer & Type:		Model:	Serial Number:
Alterations:		Capacity:	Caliber
Importer:		Barrel:	Action:

Notes:

AQUIRED	Date:	SOLD	Date:
Cost:	From:	Cost:	To:
Notes:		Notes:	

Manufacturer & Type:		Model:	Serial Number:
Alterations:		Capacity:	Caliber
Importer:		Barrel:	Action:

Notes:

AQUIRED	Date:	SOLD	Date:
Cost:	From:	Cost:	To:
Notes:		Notes:	

Manufacturer & Type:		Model:	Serial Number:
Alterations:		Capacity:	Caliber
Importer:		Barrel:	Action:

Notes:

AQUIRED	Date:	SOLD	Date:
Cost:	From:	Cost:	To:
Notes:		Notes:	

Manufacturer & Type:		Model:	Serial Number:
Alterations:		Capacity:	Caliber
Importer:		Barrel:	Action:

Notes:

AQUIRED	Date:	SOLD	Date:
Cost:	From:	Cost:	To:
Notes:		Notes:	

Manufacturer & Type:		Model:	Serial Number:
Alterations:		Capacity:	Caliber
Importer:		Barrel:	Action:

Notes:

AQUIRED	Date:	SOLD	Date:
Cost:	From:	Cost:	To:
Notes:		Notes:	

Manufacturer & Type:		Model:	Serial Number:
Alterations:		Capacity:	Caliber
Importer:		Barrel:	Action:
Notes:			

AQUIRED	Date:	SOLD	Date:
Cost:	From:	Cost:	To:
Notes:		Notes:	

Manufacturer & Type:		Model:	Serial Number:
Alterations:		Capacity:	Caliber
Importer:		Barrel:	Action:
Notes:			

AQUIRED	Date:	SOLD	Date:
Cost:	From:	Cost:	To:
Notes:		Notes:	

Manufacturer & Type:		Model:	Serial Number:
Alterations:		Capacity:	Caliber
Importer:		Barrel:	Action:
Notes:			

AQUIRED	Date:	SOLD	Date:
Cost:	From:	Cost:	To:
Notes:		Notes:	

Manufacturer & Type:		Model:	Serial Number:
Alterations:		Capacity:	Caliber
Importer:		Barrel:	Action:
Notes:			

AQUIRED	Date:	SOLD	Date:
Cost:	From:	Cost:	To:
Notes:		Notes:	

Manufacturer & Type:		Model:	Serial Number:
Alterations:		Capacity:	Caliber
Importer:		Barrel:	Action:

Notes:

AQUIRED	Date:	SOLD	Date:
Cost:	From:	Cost:	To:
Notes:		Notes:	

Manufacturer & Type:		Model:	Serial Number:
Alterations:		Capacity:	Caliber
Importer:		Barrel:	Action:

Notes:

AQUIRED	Date:	SOLD	Date:
Cost:	From:	Cost:	To:
Notes:		Notes:	

Manufacturer & Type:		Model:	Serial Number:
Alterations:		Capacity:	Caliber
Importer:		Barrel:	Action:

Notes:

AQUIRED	Date:	SOLD	Date:
Cost:	From:	Cost:	To:
Notes:		Notes:	

Manufacturer & Type:		Model:	Serial Number:
Alterations:		Capacity:	Caliber
Importer:		Barrel:	Action:

Notes:

AQUIRED	Date:	SOLD	Date:
Cost:	From:	Cost:	To:
Notes:		Notes:	

Manufacturer & Type:		Model:	Serial Number:
Alterations:		Capacity:	Caliber
Importer:		Barrel:	Action:

Notes:

AQUIRED	Date:	SOLD	Date:
Cost:	From:	Cost:	To:
Notes:		Notes:	

Manufacturer & Type:		Model:	Serial Number:
Alterations:		Capacity:	Caliber
Importer:		Barrel:	Action:

Notes:

AQUIRED	Date:	SOLD	Date:
Cost:	From:	Cost:	To:
Notes:		Notes:	

Manufacturer & Type:		Model:	Serial Number:
Alterations:		Capacity:	Caliber
Importer:		Barrel:	Action:

Notes:

AQUIRED	Date:	SOLD	Date:
Cost:	From:	Cost:	To:
Notes:		Notes:	

Manufacturer & Type:		Model:	Serial Number:
Alterations:		Capacity:	Caliber
Importer:		Barrel:	Action:

Notes:

AQUIRED	Date:	SOLD	Date:
Cost:	From:	Cost:	To:
Notes:		Notes:	

Manufacturer & Type:		Model:	Serial Number:
Alterations:		Capacity:	Caliber
Importer:		Barrel:	Action:
Notes:			

AQUIRED	Date:	SOLD	Date:
Cost:	From:	Cost:	To:
Notes:		Notes:	

Manufacturer & Type:		Model:	Serial Number:
Alterations:		Capacity:	Caliber
Importer:		Barrel:	Action:
Notes:			

AQUIRED	Date:	SOLD	Date:
Cost:	From:	Cost:	To:
Notes:		Notes:	

Manufacturer & Type:		Model:	Serial Number:
Alterations:		Capacity:	Caliber
Importer:		Barrel:	Action:

Notes:

AQUIRED	Date:	SOLD	Date:
Cost:	From:	Cost:	To:
Notes:		Notes:	

Manufacturer & Type:		Model:	Serial Number:
Alterations:		Capacity:	Caliber
Importer:		Barrel:	Action:

Notes:

AQUIRED	Date:	SOLD	Date:
Cost:	From:	Cost:	To:
Notes:		Notes:	

Manufacturer & Type:		Model:	Serial Number:
Alterations:		Capacity:	Caliber
Importer:		Barrel:	Action:

Notes:

AQUIRED	Date:	SOLD	Date:
Cost:	From:	Cost:	To:
Notes:		Notes:	

Manufacturer & Type:		Model:	Serial Number:
Alterations:		Capacity:	Caliber
Importer:		Barrel:	Action:

Notes:

AQUIRED	Date:	SOLD	Date:
Cost:	From:	Cost:	To:
Notes:		Notes:	

76

Manufacturer & Type:		Model:	Serial Number:
Alterations:		Capacity:	Caliber
Importer:		Barrel:	Action:

Notes:

AQUIRED	Date:	SOLD	Date:
Cost:	From:	Cost:	To:
Notes:		Notes:	

Manufacturer & Type:		Model:	Serial Number:
Alterations:		Capacity:	Caliber
Importer:		Barrel:	Action:

Notes:

AQUIRED	Date:	SOLD	Date:
Cost:	From:	Cost:	To:
Notes:		Notes:	

Manufacturer & Type:		Model:	Serial Number:
Alterations:		Capacity:	Caliber
Importer:		Barrel:	Action:
Notes:			

AQUIRED	Date:	SOLD	Date:
Cost:	From:	Cost:	To:
Notes:		Notes:	

Manufacturer & Type:		Model:	Serial Number:
Alterations:		Capacity:	Caliber
Importer:		Barrel:	Action:
Notes:			

AQUIRED	Date:	SOLD	Date:
Cost:	From:	Cost:	To:
Notes:		Notes:	

Manufacturer & Type:		Model:	Serial Number:
Alterations:		Capacity:	Caliber
Importer:		Barrel:	Action:

Notes:

AQUIRED	Date:	SOLD	Date:
Cost:	From:	Cost:	To:
Notes:		Notes:	

Manufacturer & Type:		Model:	Serial Number:
Alterations:		Capacity:	Caliber
Importer:		Barrel:	Action:

Notes:

AQUIRED	Date:	SOLD	Date:
Cost:	From:	Cost:	To:
Notes:		Notes:	

Manufacturer & Type:		Model:	Serial Number:
Alterations:		Capacity:	Caliber
Importer:		Barrel:	Action:
Notes:			

AQUIRED	Date:	SOLD	Date:
Cost:	From:	Cost:	To:
Notes:		Notes:	

Manufacturer & Type:		Model:	Serial Number:
Alterations:		Capacity:	Caliber
Importer:		Barrel:	Action:
Notes:			

AQUIRED	Date:	SOLD	Date:
Cost:	From:	Cost:	To:
Notes:		Notes:	

Manufacturer & Type:		Model:	Serial Number:
Alterations:		Capacity:	Caliber
Importer:		Barrel:	Action:
Notes:			

AQUIRED	Date:	SOLD	Date:
Cost:	From:	Cost:	To:
Notes:		Notes:	

Manufacturer & Type:		Model:	Serial Number:
Alterations:		Capacity:	Caliber
Importer:		Barrel:	Action:
Notes:			

AQUIRED	Date:	SOLD	Date:
Cost:	From:	Cost:	To:
Notes:		Notes:	

Manufacturer & Type:		Model:	Serial Number:
Alterations:		Capacity:	Caliber
Importer:		Barrel:	Action:
Notes:			

AQUIRED	Date:	SOLD	Date:
Cost:	From:	Cost:	To:
Notes:		Notes:	

Manufacturer & Type:		Model:	Serial Number:
Alterations:		Capacity:	Caliber
Importer:		Barrel:	Action:
Notes:			

AQUIRED	Date:	SOLD	Date:
Cost:	From:	Cost:	To:
Notes:		Notes:	

Manufacturer & Type:		Model:	Serial Number:
Alterations:		Capacity:	Caliber
Importer:		Barrel:	Action:

Notes:

AQUIRED	Date:	SOLD	Date:
Cost:	From:	Cost:	To:
Notes:		Notes:	

Manufacturer & Type:		Model:	Serial Number:
Alterations:		Capacity:	Caliber
Importer:		Barrel:	Action:

Notes:

AQUIRED	Date:	SOLD	Date:
Cost:	From:	Cost:	To:
Notes:		Notes:	

Manufacturer & Type:		Model:	Serial Number:
Alterations:		Capacity:	Caliber
Importer:		Barrel:	Action:

Notes:

AQUIRED	Date:	SOLD	Date:
Cost:	From:	Cost:	To:
Notes:		Notes:	

Manufacturer & Type:		Model:	Serial Number:
Alterations:		Capacity:	Caliber
Importer:		Barrel:	Action:

Notes:

AQUIRED	Date:	SOLD	Date:
Cost:	From:	Cost:	To:
Notes:		Notes:	

Manufacturer & Type:		Model:	Serial Number:
Alterations:		Capacity:	Caliber
Importer:		Barrel:	Action:
Notes:			

AQUIRED	Date:	SOLD	Date:
Cost:	From:	Cost:	To:
Notes:		Notes:	

Manufacturer & Type:		Model:	Serial Number:
Alterations:		Capacity:	Caliber
Importer:		Barrel:	Action:
Notes:			

AQUIRED	Date:	SOLD	Date:
Cost:	From:	Cost:	To:
Notes:		Notes:	

Manufacturer & Type:		Model:	Serial Number:
Alterations:		Capacity:	Caliber
Importer:		Barrel:	Action:
Notes:			

AQUIRED	Date:	SOLD	Date:
Cost:	From:	Cost:	To:
Notes:		Notes:	

Manufacturer & Type:		Model:	Serial Number:
Alterations:		Capacity:	Caliber
Importer:		Barrel:	Action:
Notes:			

AQUIRED	Date:	SOLD	Date:
Cost:	From:	Cost:	To:
Notes:		Notes:	

Manufacturer & Type:		Model:	Serial Number:
Alterations:		Capacity:	Caliber
Importer:		Barrel:	Action:
Notes:			

AQUIRED	Date:	SOLD	Date:
Cost:	From:	Cost:	To:
Notes:		Notes:	

Manufacturer & Type:		Model:	Serial Number:
Alterations:		Capacity:	Caliber
Importer:		Barrel:	Action:
Notes:			

AQUIRED	Date:	SOLD	Date:
Cost:	From:	Cost:	To:
Notes:		Notes:	

Manufacturer & Type:		Model:	Serial Number:
Alterations:		Capacity:	Caliber
Importer:		Barrel:	Action:

Notes:

AQUIRED	Date:	SOLD	Date:
Cost:	From:	Cost:	To:
Notes:		Notes:	

Manufacturer & Type:		Model:	Serial Number:
Alterations:		Capacity:	Caliber
Importer:		Barrel:	Action:

Notes:

AQUIRED	Date:	SOLD	Date:
Cost:	From:	Cost:	To:
Notes:		Notes:	

Manufacturer & Type:		Model:	Serial Number:
Alterations:		Capacity:	Caliber
Importer:		Barrel:	Action:

Notes:

AQUIRED	Date:	SOLD	Date:
Cost:	From:	Cost:	To:
Notes:		Notes:	

Manufacturer & Type:		Model:	Serial Number:
Alterations:		Capacity:	Caliber
Importer:		Barrel:	Action:

Notes:

AQUIRED	Date:	SOLD	Date:
Cost:	From:	Cost:	To:
Notes:		Notes:	

Notes

Notes

Notes

Notes

Notes

Notes

Notes

Notes

Notes

Notes

Notes

Notes

Notes

Notes

Notes

Notes

Notes

Notes

Notes

Notes

Notes

Notes

Notes

Notes

Notes

Notes

Notes

Notes

Notes

Notes

Notes

Made in the USA
Las Vegas, NV
05 May 2023

71602490R00069